NEW MAMA:

Realigning. Evolving. Bonding.

SET IN SOUL

ISBN #: 978-1-7321075-1-9

Published by Tatiana Media LLC

For general information on our other products and services, please contact our Customer Support within the United States at support@setinsoul.com.

Tatiana Media LLC as well as Set In Soul LLC publishes its books in a variety of electronic formats. Some content that appears in print may not be available in electronic books.

THIS JOURNAL BELONGS TO

____

DEDICATED TO EVERY NEW MOM LOOKING TO GROW HERSELF IN HER NEW JOURNEY

TABLE OF CONTENTS

HOW TO USE THIS JOURNAL

Welcome to Motherhood!!! Words cannot describe what it feels like to be a mother, or maybe they can. How does it feel? Are you getting any sleep? Silly question right? When it comes to motherhood, every mother experiences it differently. Some days you may feel ecstatic and feel love pouring down all over you. Other days your mind may be filled with thoughts and feelings you wouldn't dare share with others. Your mind may entertain thoughts where you are asking yourself the following...

- When Will This Be Over?
- Am I Cut Out For This?
- Why Is It That No One Told Me I Would Feel Like This?
- Why Do I Feel Like I Am Not Connecting?

You may even feel terrible for thinking some of your thoughts thus keeping them to yourself. Maybe you're just trying to fight off a bit of depression and some postpartum thoughts. But wait .... this may not be your experience. Everyday may be an absolute joy for you. It may be a walk in the park and you are simply looking for a place where you can document your expression of love. It is important for you to record your experiences so you can reflect back at these unforgettable moments at a later time in your life. Maybe you are feeling a mixture of both feelings. It's great one day and on another day you just can't take it. Well, this is the perfect journal for both situations. You may not have anyone you can fully talk to or even completely open up with about your feelings, but this journal is just for that. This is you talking to you. This journal is you aligning with yourself as the wonderful mother you are (whether you feel that way or not). This 'New Mama Journal' is for you to be able to take a new step into motherhood with confidence, love, and peace because you are an excellent mama.

This 'New Mama Journal' is filled with daily affirmations to affirm your position as a wonderful mother. We recommend filling out the daily prompt filled journal every night to reflect on your day as well as assess what you are improving on and your growth as a loving mother. This journal covers the first six months of motherhood to help you get through some of your most challenging times as well as record some of your funniest, most painful, lovable, and unforgettable moments. There are quotes sprinkled throughout this journal that confirm the blessing of who you are to your baby as well as what your baby is to you. Use the freestyling sections to write down your thoughts whether good or painful. Be honest with yourself. You've got this! You are a new mama who is realigning, readjusting, and connecting. Let's get started.

MOMMY PRAYERS

MOMMY PRAYERS

1. As one whom his mother comforts, so I will comfort you.
   – Isaiah 66:13

2. And Mary said: “My soul glorifies the Lord and my spirit rejoices in God my Savior, for he has been mindful of the humble state of his servant. From now on all generations will call me blessed.”
   – Luke 1:46-48

3. Blessed are all who fear the LORD, who walk in obedience to him. You will eat the fruit of your labor; blessings and prosperity will be yours. - Psalm 128:1-2

4. May the LORD bless you from Zion; may you see the prosperity of Jerusalem all the days of your life. May you live to see your children’s children — peace be on Israel. - Psalm 128:5-6

5. You, God, are my God, earnestly I seek you; I thirst for you, my whole being longs for you, in a dry and parched land where there is no water. – Psalm 63:1

6. Praise be to the Lord, to God our Savior, who daily bears our burdens. – Psalm 68:19

7. When they saw the courage of Peter and John and realized that they were unschooled, ordinary men, they were astonished and they took note that these men had been with Jesus. – Acts 4:13

8. As you do not know the path of the wind, or how the body is formed in a mother’s womb, so you cannot understand the work of God, the Maker of all things. – Ecclesiastes 11:5

9. Children are a heritage from the LORD, offspring a reward from him. Like arrows in the hands of a warrior are children born in one’s youth. Blessed is the man whose quiver is full of them.

They will not be put to shame when they contend with their opponents in court. – Psalm 127:3-5

10. God is within her, she will not fall; God will help her at break of day. – Psalm 46:5

11. Trust in him at all times, O people; pour out your heart before him; God is a refuge for us. – Psalm 62:8

12. The Lord is my strength and my shield; my heart trusts in him, and I am helped. – Psalm 28:7

13. Don't worry about anything, but in everything, through prayer and petition with thanksgiving, present your requests to God. And the peace of God, which surpasses all understanding, will guard your hearts and minds in Christ Jesus. – Philippians 4:6-7

14. Come with Me by yourselves to a quiet place and get some rest. – Mark 6:31

15. But those who hope in the LORD will renew their strength. They will soar on wings like eagles; they will run and not grow weary, they will walk and not be faint. – Isaiah 40:31

16. And let us not be weary in well doing: for in due season we shall reap, if we faint not. – Galatians 6:9

17. For his anger endureth but a moment; in his favour is life: weeping may endure for a night, but joy cometh in the morning. – Psalm 30:5

18. Humble yourselves therefore under the mighty hand of God, that he may exalt you in due time: Casting all your care upon him; for he careth for you. – 1 Peter 5:6-7

MY BABY'S FIRSTS

MY BABY'S FIRSTS

The First Time My Baby Smiled:

The First Time I Heard My Baby Laugh:

The First Sounds My Baby Made:

The First Time My Baby Got Sick:

My Baby's First Doctor Visit After Giving Birth:

MY BABY'S FIRSTS

The First Time My Baby Controlled And Lifted His/Her Head:

My Baby's First Bath:

The First Time My Baby Rolled Over:

The First Time My Baby Sat Up:

The First Solid Foods My Baby Ate:

MY BABY'S FIRSTS

The First Time My Baby Started Reaching For Things:

The First Time My Baby Started Grabbing Things:

My Baby's First Trip Out:

My Baby's First Holiday:

The First Time My Baby Started Experiencing Teething Pains:

MY BABY'S FIRSTS

The First Word My Baby Said:

MY FIRSTS

MY FIRSTS

The First Thing I Ate After Giving Birth:

The First Time I Was Able To Fit Back Into My Favorite Dress After Giving Birth:

The First Time I Was Able To Fit Back Into My Favorite Shoes Again After Giving Birth:

The First Time I Was Able To Get A Few Hours Of Sleep After Giving Birth:

The First Time I Was Able To Successfully Breastfeed (If Applicable):

MY FIRSTS

The First Time I Was Able To Set Up A Routine After Giving Birth:

The First Time I Was Able To Hang Out With My Friends After Giving Birth:

The First Time I Was Able To Watch A Movie After Giving Birth:

The First Alcoholic Drink I Was Able To Have After Giving Birth (Answer If Applicable - If Not Breastfeeding):

The First Time I Noticed I Was Losing Weight After Giving Birth:

MY FIRSTS

The First Time I Noticed Excessive Hair Shedding After Giving Birth:

The First Time I Was Able To Sleep On My Stomach Comfortably After Giving Birth:

The First Time I Was Able To Eat Sushi After Giving Birth:

The First Meal I Was Able To Cook After Giving Birth:

BABY BLUES

BABY BLUES

I Feel Sensitive About:

I Seem To Cry Over:

I'm Always Close To Tears When:

I Feel Irritable About:

I Get Anxious About:

BABY BLUES

I Am Unmotivated About:

I Am Worried About:

I Feel Odd About:

When I Am Not Connecting, Feeling The Bond Or Love Towards My Baby, It Makes Me Feel (Answer If Applicable):

Some Mood Swings I Am Experiencing:

BABY BLUES

I Need Understanding In:

I Believe I Need Support In:

NEW MAMA QUESTIONS

NEW MAMA QUESTIONS

Home Birth Or Hospital Birth?

Vaginal Birth Or C-Section?

As A New Mom, I Feel:

As A New Mom, I Am Surprised:

As A New Mom, I Didn't Expect:

NEW MAMA QUESTIONS

No One Told Me:

I Am Happy:

Do I Want More Kids?

I Tend To Forget:

My Body Feels:

NEW MAMA QUESTIONS

Holding My Baby For The First Time Felt:

Feeding My Baby For The First Time Felt:

My First Thought When I First Saw My Baby:

The First Night With My Baby:

Bringing My Baby Home From The Hospital Felt:

NEW MAMA QUESTIONS

I Would Describe My Birthing Experience:

I Would Describe My Newborn:

When I Gave Birth, These People Were There (Write Down Everyone Who Was There):

For The First Few Days:

My Pet(s) Responded To Having A Newborn In Our Home By:
(Answer If Applicable):

NEW MAMA QUESTIONS

The People That Were There With Me The First Few Days/Weeks To Help Me With My Newborn:

The Best Baby Gifts Were:

I Believe My Baby Looks Like:

I Feel Like My Baby:

My Relationship With My Mother Since Having My Baby (Answer If Applicable):

NEW MAMA QUESTIONS

The Relationship With My Significant Other/Husband/Baby's Father Since Having My Baby:

I Need To Make Time For:

I Need Time To:

Things I Have Unintentionally Stopped Doing:

What Inspires Me?

NEW MAMA QUESTIONS

Some Unhealthy Practices I Keep Doing:

Negative Thoughts I Keep Having:

Positive Thoughts I Keep Close To Me:

I Look Forward To:

I Relax When:

NEW MAMA QUESTIONS

I Don't Feel Prepared For:

I Didn't Feel Prepared For:

I Fear:

I Get Anxiety When:

I Fight With Myself About:

NEW MAMA QUESTIONS

Sometimes I Feel Like I Failed At:

Why (In Regards To The Response From The Prompt Above)?

I Get Frustrated When:

I Cry About:

My Life Use To Be:

NEW MAMA QUESTIONS

Now My Life Is:

I Want To Say No To:

I Want To Say Yes To:

I Emotionally Feel:

My Productivity Level:

NEW MAMA QUESTIONS

I Can't Wait Until My Baby:

Every Time My Baby Looks At Me, I:

When My Baby Cries, I Feel:

I Don't Have Time To:

I Will Make Time To:

NEW MAMA QUESTIONS

I Am Doing My Best At:

I Am Grateful:

I Could Really Use:

My Job/Career/Schooling:

I Am Recovering From:

NEW MAMA QUESTIONS

I Will Always Remember:

One Thing I Wish I Could've Done Differently:

Drama I Am Staying Away From:

I Notice:

I Wish It Was Okay To:

NEW MAMA QUESTIONS

I Choose Not To Feel Bad About:

I Made The Decision To:

A Great Day For Me Looks Like:

I Consider A Successful Day To Be:

My Baby's Biggest Struggle:

NEW MAMA QUESTIONS

My Greatest Strength As A Mom:

I Hope My Baby Sees Me And Thinks:

My Baby Counts On Me To:

My Baby And I Spend Time Together By:

The Hardest Part About Being A Mom Is:

NEW MAMA QUESTIONS

The Easiest Part About Being A Mom Is:

It's Okay That I Am:

I Noticed That My Friends:

I Noticed That My Family:

I Wish My Partner Would (Answer If Applicable):

NEW MAMA QUESTIONS

Everyday Feels Like:

When I See Other Moms, I Feel:

I Know There Will Be A Time When:

I Can't Wait To Catch Up With:

I Prepared For Motherhood By:

NEW MAMA QUESTIONS

This Pregnancy Was Different Because (Answer If Applicable):

I Am Trying To Adjust To:

The Thoughts That Run Through My Mind:

Some Of My Next Purchases Will Be:

Some Challenges I Am Facing:

NEW MAMA QUESTIONS

I Know In Due Time I:

I Feel Like I Am Getting Better At:

What Wasn't Important To Me Before That Is Important To Me Now:

What Was Important To Me Before That Is No Longer Important To Me Now:

I Am Now Interested In:

NEW MAMA QUESTIONS

I Find Myself Talking A Lot About:

I Enjoy:

I Can Do A Better Job At:

I Now Have Peace Knowing:

I Currently Believe I Look:

NEW MAMA QUESTIONS

I Will Overcome:

When I'm Away From My Baby, I Feel:

I Take Pride In:

When Nothing Seems To Be Going Right, I:

I Laugh Knowing:

NEW MAMA QUESTIONS

I Needed To Get Out:

I Always Dreamed Motherhood Would Be:

What Motherhood Actually Is To Me:

My Baby And I Are:

I Am Starting To Relax About:

NEW MAMA QUESTIONS

As A New Mom, I:

What I Would Do Differently With My Next Kid (Answer If Applicable):

Complications I Experienced While Giving Birth:

Complications I Am Experiencing Now:

FIRST 60 DAYS:

REALIGNING COMPLETELY

FIRST 60 DAYS: REALIGNING COMPLETELY

Date:

Mood:

I Feel:

Today's Story:

I Need:

I Loved On Myself Today By:

Today Was:

Today's Nagging Thought:

My Baby:

What My Baby Did Today:

FIRST 60 DAYS: REALIGNING COMPLETELY

Date:

Mood:

I Feel:

Today's Story:

I Need:

I Loved On Myself Today By:

Today Was:

Today's Nagging Thought:

My Baby:

What My Baby Did Today:

FIRST 60 DAYS: REALIGNING COMPLETELY

Date:

Mood:

I Feel:

Today's Story:

I Need:

I Loved On Myself Today By:

Today Was:

Today's Nagging Thought:

My Baby:

What My Baby Did Today:

FIRST 60 DAYS: REALIGNING COMPLETELY

Date:

Mood:

I Feel:

Today's Story:

I Need:

I Loved On Myself Today By:

Today Was:

Today's Nagging Thought:

My Baby:

What My Baby Did Today:

I Am Confident In My Maternal Intuition. I Know That It Can Help Me Mold My Child To Be The Best That He/She Can Be.

FIRST 60 DAYS: REALIGNING COMPLETELY

Date:

Mood:

I Feel:

I Need:

Today Was:

My Baby:

Today's Story:

I Loved On Myself Today By:

Today's Nagging Thought:

What My Baby Did Today:

NEW MAMA THOUGHTS

FIRST 60 DAYS: REALIGNING COMPLETELY

Date:

Mood:

I Feel:

I Need:

Today Was:

My Baby:

Today's Story:

I Loved On Myself Today By:

Today's Nagging Thought:

What My Baby Did Today:

FIRST 60 DAYS: REALIGNING COMPLETELY

Date: Mood:

I Feel:

Today's Story:

I Need:

I Loved On Myself Today By:

Today Was:

Today's Nagging Thought:

My Baby:

What My Baby Did Today:

Nothing
Is More
Important
To Me
Than You.
- God

My Comeback Will Be Amazing.

FIRST 60 DAYS: REALIGNING COMPLETELY

Date:

Mood:

I Feel:

I Need:

Today Was:

My Baby:

Today's Story:

I Loved On Myself Today By:

Today's Nagging Thought:

What My Baby Did Today:

FIRST 60 DAYS: REALIGNING COMPLETELY

Date:

Mood:

I Feel:

I Need:

Today Was:

My Baby:

Today's Story:

I Loved On Myself Today By:

Today's Nagging Thought:

What My Baby Did Today:

FIRST 60 DAYS: REALIGNING COMPLETELY

Date:

I Feel:

I Need:

Today Was:

My Baby:

Mood:

Today's Story:

I Loved On Myself Today By:

Today's Nagging Thought:

What My Baby Did Today:

My One Goal Today....

FIRST 60 DAYS: REALIGNING COMPLETELY

Date:

Mood:

I Feel:

Today's Story:

I Need:

I Loved On Myself Today By:

Today Was:

Today's Nagging Thought:

My Baby:

What My Baby Did Today:

FIRST 60 DAYS: REALIGNING COMPLETELY

Date:

Mood:

I Feel:

Today's Story:

I Need:

I Loved On Myself Today By:

Today Was:

Today's Nagging Thought:

My Baby:

What My Baby Did Today:

FIRST 60 DAYS: REALIGNING COMPLETELY

Date:

Mood:

I Feel:

Today's Story:

I Need:

I Loved On Myself Today By:

Today Was:

Today's Nagging Thought:

My Baby:

What My Baby Did Today:

NEW MAMA THOUGHTS

I Can Make It Through The Good, Bad, And Messy Days.

Mom
Wow
Mom
Wow
Mom
Wow
Mom
Wow

FIRST 60 DAYS: REALIGNING COMPLETELY

Date:

Mood:

I Feel:

Today's Story:

I Need:

I Loved On Myself Today By:

Today Was:

Today's Nagging Thought:

My Baby:

What My Baby Did Today:

FIRST 60 DAYS: REALIGNING COMPLETELY

Date:

Mood:

I Feel:

Today's Story:

I Need:

I Loved On Myself Today By:

Today Was:

Today's Nagging Thought:

My Baby:

What My Baby Did Today:

FIRST 60 DAYS: REALIGNING COMPLETELY

Date:

Mood:

I Feel:

Today's Story:

I Need:

I Loved On Myself Today By:

Today Was:

Today's Nagging Thought:

My Baby:

What My Baby Did Today:

My Body Goals Are....

FIRST 60 DAYS: REALIGNING COMPLETELY

Date:

Mood:

I Feel:

Today's Story:

I Need:

I Loved On Myself Today By:

Today Was:

Today's Nagging Thought:

My Baby:

What My Baby Did Today:

FIRST 60 DAYS: REALIGNING COMPLETELY

Date:

Mood:

I Feel:

Today's Story:

I Need:

I Loved On Myself Today By:

Today Was:

Today's Nagging Thought:

My Baby:

What My Baby Did Today:

FIRST 60 DAYS: REALIGNING COMPLETELY

Date:

Mood:

I Feel:

Today's Story:

I Need:

I Loved On Myself Today By:

Today Was:

Today's Nagging Thought:

My Baby:

What My Baby Did Today:

Ma.
Mom.
Mommy.
Mama.
Mum.
Mummy.

NEW MAMA THOUGHTS

FIRST 60 DAYS: REALIGNING COMPLETELY

Date:

Mood:

I Feel:

I Need:

Today Was:

My Baby:

Today's Story:

I Loved On Myself Today By:

Today's Nagging Thought:

What My Baby Did Today:

FIRST 60 DAYS: REALIGNING COMPLETELY

Date:

Mood:

I Feel:

Today's Story:

I Need:

I Loved On Myself Today By:

Today Was:

Today's Nagging Thought:

My Baby:

What My Baby Did Today:

FIRST 60 DAYS: REALIGNING COMPLETELY

Date:

Mood:

I Feel:

Today's Story:

I Need:

I Loved On Myself Today By:

Today Was:

Today's Nagging Thought:

My Baby:

What My Baby Did Today:

Being A Mom
Is A Lifetime
Position That
I Am Happy
To Have.

I Believe My Child Is God's Way Of Teaching Me What Real Love Is.

FIRST 60 DAYS: REALIGNING COMPLETELY

Date:

Mood:

I Feel:

Today's Story:

I Need:

I Loved On Myself Today By:

Today Was:

Today's Nagging Thought:

My Baby:

What My Baby Did Today:

FIRST 60 DAYS: REALIGNING COMPLETELY

I Am Truly Grateful For My Body And Its Ability To Create Life.

Date:

Mood:

I Feel:

Today's Story:

I Need:

I Loved On Myself Today By:

Today Was:

Today's Nagging Thought:

My Baby:

What My Baby Did Today:

NEW MAMA THOUGHTS

FIRST 60 DAYS: REALIGNING COMPLETELY

Date:

Mood:

I Feel:

I Need:

Today Was:

My Baby:

Today's Story:

I Loved On Myself Today By:

Today's Nagging Thought:

What My Baby Did Today:

I Am Excited To Play And Fulfill A Lot Of Roles In My Baby's Life.

FIRST 60 DAYS: REALIGNING COMPLETELY

Date:

Mood:

I Feel:

Today's Story:

I Need:

I Loved On Myself Today By:

Today Was:

Today's Nagging Thought:

My Baby:

What My Baby Did Today:

FIRST 60 DAYS: REALIGNING COMPLETELY

Date:

Mood:

I Feel:

Today's Story:

I Need:

I Loved On Myself Today By:

Today Was:

Today's Nagging Thought:

My Baby:

What My Baby Did Today:

Five Words I Would Say Motherhood Is Right Now....

FIRST 60 DAYS: REALIGNING COMPLETELY

Date:

Mood:

I Feel:

Today's Story:

I Need:

I Loved On Myself Today By:

Today Was:

Today's Nagging Thought:

My Baby:

What My Baby Did Today:

FIRST 60 DAYS: REALIGNING COMPLETELY

Date:

Mood:

I Feel:

Today's Story:

I Need:

I Loved On Myself Today By:

Today Was:

Today's Nagging Thought:

My Baby:

What My Baby Did Today:

FIRST 60 DAYS: REALIGNING COMPLETELY

Date:

Mood:

I Feel:

Today's Story:

I Need:

I Loved On Myself Today By:

Today Was:

Today's Nagging Thought:

My Baby:

What My Baby Did Today:

FIRST 60 DAYS: REALIGNING COMPLETELY

Date:

Mood:

I Feel:

Today's Story:

I Need:

I Loved On Myself Today By:

Today Was:

Today's Nagging Thought:

My Baby:

What My Baby Did Today:

I Am Capable Of Showering My Baby With The Love And Affection He/She Needs.

NEW MAMA THOUGHTS

No Negative
Thought
Will Keep
Me Away
From My
Baby.

FIRST 60 DAYS: REALIGNING COMPLETELY

Date:

Mood:

I Feel:

Today's Story:

I Need:

I Loved On Myself Today By:

Today Was:

Today's Nagging Thought:

My Baby:

What My Baby Did Today:

FIRST 60 DAYS: REALIGNING COMPLETELY

Date:

Mood:

I Feel:

Today's Story:

I Need:

I Loved On Myself Today By:

Today Was:

Today's Nagging Thought:

My Baby:

What My Baby Did Today:

FIRST 60 DAYS: REALIGNING COMPLETELY

Date:

Mood:

I Feel:

Today's Story:

I Need:

I Loved On Myself Today By:

Today Was:

Today's Nagging Thought:

My Baby:

What My Baby Did Today:

FIRST 60 DAYS: REALIGNING COMPLETELY

Date:

Mood:

I Feel:

Today's Story:

I Need:

I Loved On Myself Today By:

Today Was:

Today's Nagging Thought:

My Baby:

What My Baby Did Today:

Prayers That Help Me To Push Forward....

NEW MAMA THOUGHTS

FIRST 60 DAYS: REALIGNING COMPLETELY

Date:

Mood:

I Feel:

I Need:

Today Was:

My Baby:

Today's Story:

I Loved On Myself Today By:

Today's Nagging Thought:

What My Baby Did Today:

I Will Always Be A Witness To My Baby's Small And Huge Milestones.

In Every Way, My Child Is Beautiful.

FIRST 60 DAYS: REALIGNING COMPLETELY

Date:

Mood:

I Feel:

I Need:

Today Was:

My Baby:

Today's Story:

I Loved On Myself Today By:

Today's Nagging Thought:

What My Baby Did Today:

FIRST 60 DAYS: REALIGNING COMPLETELY

Date: | Mood:

I Feel:

Today's Story:

I Need:

I Loved On Myself Today By:

Today Was:

Today's Nagging Thought:

My Baby:

What My Baby Did Today:

FIRST 60 DAYS: REALIGNING COMPLETELY

Date:

Mood:

I Feel:

Today's Story:

I Need:

I Loved On Myself Today By:

Today Was:

Today's Nagging Thought:

My Baby:

What My Baby Did Today:

I Am Proud Of My Baby's Accomplishments.

FIRST 60 DAYS: REALIGNING COMPLETELY

Date:

Mood:

I Feel:

I Need:

Today Was:

My Baby:

Today's Story:

I Loved On Myself Today By:

Today's Nagging Thought:

What My Baby Did Today:

When I Breastfeed, I....

FIRST 60 DAYS: REALIGNING COMPLETELY

Date:

Mood:

I Feel:

Today's Story:

I Need:

I Loved On Myself Today By:

Today Was:

Today's Nagging Thought:

My Baby:

What My Baby Did Today:

FIRST 60 DAYS: REALIGNING COMPLETELY

Date:

Mood:

I Feel:

Today's Story:

I Need:

I Loved On Myself Today By:

Today Was:

Today's Nagging Thought:

My Baby:

What My Baby Did Today:

I Am Capable Of Fulfilling My Purpose As A Mother.

One Of The Ways
I Express Love
To Myself Is
By Taking Deep
Breaths And
Telling Myself....
All That I Need I
Have Within Me.

My Baby And I Wear Crowns Over Here.

FIRST 60 DAYS: REALIGNING COMPLETELY

Date:

Mood:

I Feel:

Today's Story:

I Need:

I Loved On Myself Today By:

Today Was:

Today's Nagging Thought:

My Baby:

What My Baby Did Today:

I Am Energetic And Healthy. I Enjoy My Daily Activities As A Mom.

FIRST 60 DAYS: REALIGNING COMPLETELY

Date:

Mood:

I Feel:

I Need:

Today Was:

My Baby:

Today's Story:

I Loved On Myself Today By:

Today's Nagging Thought:

What My Baby Did Today:

NEW MAMA THOUGHTS

I Am A Good Mom Who Is Filled With The Light Of Love, Happiness, And Peace.

FIRST 60 DAYS: REALIGNING COMPLETELY

Date:

Mood:

I Feel:

Today's Story:

I Need:

I Loved On Myself Today By:

Today Was:

Today's Nagging Thought:

My Baby:

What My Baby Did Today:

FIRST 60 DAYS: REALIGNING COMPLETELY

Date:

Mood:

I Feel:

Today's Story:

I Need:

I Loved On Myself Today By:

Today Was:

Today's Nagging Thought:

My Baby:

What My Baby Did Today:

I Am Capable Of Nurturing Myself And Taking Care Of My Needs.

FIRST 60 DAYS: REALIGNING COMPLETELY

Date:

Mood:

I Feel:

I Need:

Today Was:

My Baby:

Today's Story:

I Loved On Myself Today By:

Today's Nagging Thought:

What My Baby Did Today:

FIRST 60 DAYS: REALIGNING COMPLETELY

Date:

Mood:

I Feel:

I Need:

Today Was:

My Baby:

Today's Story:

I Loved On Myself Today By:

Today's Nagging Thought:

What My Baby Did Today:

I Am Surrounded By Loving People Who Support Me.

When My Baby Looks At Me, I....

This Is
One Job
I Choose
Never
To Retire
From.

FIRST 60 DAYS: REALIGNING COMPLETELY

Date:

Mood:

I Feel:

Today's Story:

I Need:

I Loved On Myself Today By:

Today Was:

Today's Nagging Thought:

My Baby:

What My Baby Did Today:

I Deserve Private Time Alone.

FIRST 60 DAYS: REALIGNING COMPLETELY

Date: Mood:

I Feel:	Today's Story:
I Need:	I Loved On Myself Today By:
Today Was:	Today's Nagging Thought:
My Baby:	What My Baby Did Today:

FIRST 60 DAYS: REALIGNING COMPLETELY

Date:

Mood:

I Feel:

I Need:

Today Was:

My Baby:

Today's Story:

I Loved On Myself Today By:

Today's Nagging Thought:

What My Baby Did Today:

I Feel 'At Peace' When I....

FIRST 60 DAYS: REALIGNING COMPLETELY

Date:

Mood:

I Feel:

Today's Story:

I Need:

I Loved On Myself Today By:

Today Was:

Today's Nagging Thought:

My Baby:

What My Baby Did Today:

FIRST 60 DAYS: REALIGNING COMPLETELY

Date:

Mood:

I Feel:

I Need:

Today Was:

My Baby:

Today's Story:

I Loved On Myself Today By:

Today's Nagging Thought:

What My Baby Did Today:

FIRST 60 DAYS: REALIGNING COMPLETELY

Date:

Mood:

I Feel:

Today's Story:

I Need:

I Loved On Myself Today By:

Today Was:

Today's Nagging Thought:

My Baby:

What My Baby Did Today:

I'm Allowed To Be A Super Mom And A Super Woman And Still Be Super Tired.

Everyday My Best Is Different. I Am Okay With That.

FIRST 60 DAYS: REALIGNING COMPLETELY

Date: | Mood:

I Feel:

I Need:

Today Was:

My Baby:

Today's Story:

I Loved On Myself Today By:

Today's Nagging Thought:

What My Baby Did Today:

FIRST 60 DAYS: REALIGNING COMPLETELY

Date:

Mood:

I Feel:

I Need:

Today Was:

My Baby:

Today's Story:

I Loved On Myself Today By:

Today's Nagging Thought:

What My Baby Did Today:

My First Holiday As A Mom, I Planned....

I Love That I....

FIRST 60 DAYS: REALIGNING COMPLETELY

Date:

Mood:

I Feel:

Today's Story:

I Need:

I Loved On Myself Today By:

Today Was:

Today's Nagging Thought:

My Baby:

What My Baby Did Today:

FIRST 60 DAYS: REALIGNING COMPLETELY

Date:

Mood:

I Feel:

Today's Story:

I Need:

I Loved On Myself Today By:

Today Was:

Today's Nagging Thought:

My Baby:

What My Baby Did Today:

FIRST 60 DAYS: REALIGNING COMPLETELY

Date:

Mood:

I Feel:

I Need:

Today Was:

My Baby:

Today's Story:

I Loved On Myself Today By:

Today's Nagging Thought:

What My Baby Did Today:

FIRST 60 DAYS: REALIGNING COMPLETELY

Date:

Mood:

I Feel:

Today's Story:

I Need:

I Loved On Myself Today By:

Today Was:

Today's Nagging Thought:

My Baby:

What My Baby Did Today:

I'm Excited To Reinvent Myself.

FIRST 60 DAYS: REALIGNING COMPLETELY

Date:

Mood:

I Feel:

I Need:

Today Was:

My Baby:

Today's Story:

I Loved On Myself Today By:

Today's Nagging Thought:

What My Baby Did Today:

NEW MAMA THOUGHTS

FIRST 60 DAYS: REALIGNING COMPLETELY

Date:

Mood:

I Feel:

Today's Story:

I Need:

I Loved On Myself Today By:

Today Was:

Today's Nagging Thought:

My Baby:

What My Baby Did Today:

THE NEXT 60 DAYS:

I'M EVOLVING

THE NEXT 60 DAYS: I'M EVOLVING

Date:

Mood:

I Feel:

Today I Figured Out:

My Body Needs:

I Know I Can:

Today I Prayed:

I Am Getting Better At:

Today Was:

Today's Compliment To Myself:

Today's Story:

My Baby:

THE NEXT 60 DAYS: I'M EVOLVING

Date:

Mood:

I Feel:

I Am Getting Better At:

Today I Figured Out:

Today Was:

My Body Needs:

Today's Compliment To Myself:

I Know I Can:

Today's Story:

Today I Prayed:

My Baby:

THE NEXT 60 DAYS: I'M EVOLVING

Date:

Mood:

I Feel:

Today I Figured Out:

My Body Needs:

I Know I Can:

Today I Prayed:

I Am Getting Better At:

Today Was:

Today's Compliment To Myself:

Today's Story:

My Baby:

I No Longer
Ask If I'm
Good Enough.
I Now Just
Ask If It's
Good For Us.

NEW MAMA THOUGHTS

THE NEXT 60 DAYS: I'M EVOLVING

Date:

Mood:

I Feel:

Today I Figured Out:

My Body Needs:

I Know I Can:

Today I Prayed:

I Am Getting Better At:

Today Was:

Today's Compliment To Myself:

Today's Story:

My Baby:

THE NEXT 60 DAYS: I'M EVOLVING

Date:

Mood:

I Feel:

Today I Figured Out:

My Body Needs:

I Know I Can:

Today I Prayed:

I Am Getting Better At:

Today Was:

Today's Compliment To Myself:

Today's Story:

My Baby:

THE NEXT 60 DAYS: I'M EVOLVING

Date:

Mood:

I Feel:

I Am Getting Better At:

Today I Figured Out:

Today Was:

My Body Needs:

Today's Compliment To Myself:

I Know I Can:

Today's Story:

Today I Prayed:

My Baby:

I'm Not Going Crazy. All Of This Is Normal. It's All A Part Of The Process.

I Can't Even Wake Up Angry Because My Baby Makes Me Smile.

THE NEXT 60 DAYS: I'M EVOLVING

Date:

Mood:

I Feel:

Today I Figured Out:

My Body Needs:

I Know I Can:

Today I Prayed:

I Am Getting Better At:

Today Was:

Today's Compliment To Myself:

Today's Story:

My Baby:

THE NEXT 60 DAYS: I'M EVOLVING

Date:

Mood:

I Feel:

Today I Figured Out:

My Body Needs:

I Know I Can:

Today I Prayed:

I Am Getting Better At:

Today Was:

Today's Compliment To Myself:

Today's Story:

My Baby:

NEW MAMA THOUGHTS

THE NEXT 60 DAYS: I'M EVOLVING

Date:

Mood:

I Feel:

I Am Getting Better At:

Today I Figured Out:

Today Was:

My Body Needs:

Today's Compliment To Myself:

I Know I Can:

Today's Story:

Today I Prayed:

My Baby:

THE NEXT 60 DAYS: I'M EVOLVING

Date:

Mood:

I Feel:

Today I Figured Out:

My Body Needs:

I Know I Can:

Today I Prayed:

I Am Getting Better At:

Today Was:

Today's Compliment To Myself:

Today's Story:

My Baby:

THE NEXT 60 DAYS: I'M EVOLVING

Date:

Mood:

I Feel:

I Am Getting Better At:

Today I Figured Out:

Today Was:

My Body Needs:

Today's Compliment To Myself:

I Know I Can:

Today's Story:

Today I Prayed:

My Baby:

THE NEXT 60 DAYS: I'M EVOLVING

Date:

Mood:

I Feel:

Today I Figured Out:

My Body Needs:

I Know I Can:

Today I Prayed:

I Am Getting Better At:

Today Was:

Today's Compliment To Myself:

Today's Story:

My Baby:

If I Could Do Anything And Go Anywhere Right Now, I Would Go....

I Appreciate My Mother Even More.

THE NEXT 60 DAYS: I'M EVOLVING

Date:

Mood:

I Feel:

I Am Getting Better At:

Today I Figured Out:

Today Was:

My Body Needs:

Today's Compliment To Myself:

I Know I Can:

Today's Story:

Today I Prayed:

My Baby:

THE NEXT 60 DAYS: I'M EVOLVING

Date:

Mood:

I Feel:

Today I Figured Out:

My Body Needs:

I Know I Can:

Today I Prayed:

I Am Getting Better At:

Today Was:

Today's Compliment To Myself:

Today's Story:

My Baby:

20 Things I Am Grateful For....

1.

2.

3.

4.

5.

6.

7.

8.

9.

10.

11.

12.

13.

14.

15.

16.

17.

18.

19.

20.

THE NEXT 60 DAYS: I'M EVOLVING

Date:

Mood:

I Feel:

Today I Figured Out:

My Body Needs:

I Know I Can:

Today I Prayed:

I Am Getting Better At:

Today Was:

Today's Compliment To Myself:

Today's Story:

My Baby:

THE NEXT 60 DAYS: I'M EVOLVING

Date:

Mood:

I Feel:

I Am Getting Better At:

Today I Figured Out:

Today Was:

My Body Needs:

Today's Compliment To Myself:

I Know I Can:

Today's Story:

Today I Prayed:

My Baby:

I Can Push Through All The Challenges Of Motherhood And Use Them To Become Better.

THE NEXT 60 DAYS: I'M EVOLVING

Date:

Mood:

I Feel:

Today I Figured Out:

My Body Needs:

I Know I Can:

Today I Prayed:

I Am Getting Better At:

Today Was:

Today's Compliment To Myself:

Today's Story:

My Baby:

It Only Gets Better From Here.

THE NEXT 60 DAYS: I'M EVOLVING

Date:

Mood:

I Feel:

Today I Figured Out:

My Body Needs:

I Know I Can:

Today I Prayed:

I Am Getting Better At:

Today Was:

Today's Compliment To Myself:

Today's Story:

My Baby:

THE NEXT 60 DAYS: I'M EVOLVING

Date:

Mood:

I Feel:

I Am Getting Better At:

Today I Figured Out:

Today Was:

My Body Needs:

Today's Compliment To Myself:

I Know I Can:

Today's Story:

Today I Prayed:

My Baby:

I Will Cherish
This Time
In My Life
Because I
Prayed So
Much To
Have This.

I'm Starting To Feel Okay In Not Knowing. I Have Faith That It Will All Work Out And That I Will Learn Along The Way.

THE NEXT 60 DAYS: I'M EVOLVING

Date:

Mood:

I Feel:

Today I Figured Out:

My Body Needs:

I Know I Can:

Today I Prayed:

I Am Getting Better At:

Today Was:

Today's Compliment To Myself:

Today's Story:

My Baby:

THE NEXT 60 DAYS: I'M EVOLVING

Date:

Mood:

I Feel:

I Am Getting Better At:

Today I Figured Out:

Today Was:

My Body Needs:

Today's Compliment To Myself:

I Know I Can:

Today's Story:

Today I Prayed:

My Baby:

NEW MAMA THOUGHTS

THE NEXT 60 DAYS: I'M EVOLVING

Date:

Mood:

I Feel:

Today I Figured Out:

My Body Needs:

I Know I Can:

Today I Prayed:

I Am Getting Better At:

Today Was:

Today's Compliment To Myself:

Today's Story:

My Baby:

THE NEXT 60 DAYS: I'M EVOLVING

Date:

Mood:

I Feel:

Today I Figured Out:

My Body Needs:

I Know I Can:

Today I Prayed:

I Am Getting Better At:

Today Was:

Today's Compliment To Myself:

Today's Story:

My Baby:

THE NEXT 60 DAYS: I'M EVOLVING

Date:

Mood:

I Feel:

I Am Getting Better At:

Today I Figured Out:

Today Was:

My Body Needs:

Today's Compliment To Myself:

I Know I Can:

Today's Story:

Today I Prayed:

My Baby:

I Am
100%
Enough.

I Am Healing Well. Inside And Out.

THE NEXT 60 DAYS: I'M EVOLVING

Date:

Mood:

I Feel:

Today I Figured Out:

My Body Needs:

I Know I Can:

Today I Prayed:

I Am Getting Better At:

Today Was:

Today's Compliment To Myself:

Today's Story:

My Baby:

THE NEXT 60 DAYS: I'M EVOLVING

Date:

Mood:

I Feel:

Today I Figured Out:

My Body Needs:

I Know I Can:

Today I Prayed:

I Am Getting Better At:

Today Was:

Today's Compliment To Myself:

Today's Story:

My Baby:

NEW MAMA THOUGHTS

THE NEXT 60 DAYS: I'M EVOLVING

Date:

Mood:

I Feel:

Today I Figured Out:

My Body Needs:

I Know I Can:

Today I Prayed:

I Am Getting Better At:

Today Was:

Today's Compliment To Myself:

Today's Story:

My Baby:

THE NEXT 60 DAYS: I'M EVOLVING

Date:

Mood:

I Feel:

I Am Getting Better At:

Today I Figured Out:

Today Was:

My Body Needs:

Today's Compliment To Myself:

I Know I Can:

Today's Story:

Today I Prayed:

My Baby:

Right Now My Home Feels....

I Would Like My Home To Feel....

THE NEXT 60 DAYS: I'M EVOLVING

Date:

Mood:

I Feel:

Today I Figured Out:

My Body Needs:

I Know I Can:

Today I Prayed:

I Am Getting Better At:

Today Was:

Today's Compliment To Myself:

Today's Story:

My Baby:

THE NEXT 60 DAYS: I'M EVOLVING

Date:

Mood:

I Feel:

Today I Figured Out:

My Body Needs:

I Know I Can:

Today I Prayed:

I Am Getting Better At:

Today Was:

Today's Compliment To Myself:

Today's Story:

My Baby:

THE NEXT 60 DAYS: I'M EVOLVING

Date:

Mood:

I Feel:

Today I Figured Out:

My Body Needs:

I Know I Can:

Today I Prayed:

I Am Getting Better At:

Today Was:

Today's Compliment To Myself:

Today's Story:

My Baby:

I Release My Need To Impress Others. I Am An Excellent Mom.

THE NEXT 60 DAYS: I'M EVOLVING

Date:

Mood:

I Feel:

Today I Figured Out:

My Body Needs:

I Know I Can:

Today I Prayed:

I Am Getting Better At:

Today Was:

Today's Compliment To Myself:

Today's Story:

My Baby:

THE NEXT 60 DAYS: I'M EVOLVING

Date:

Mood:

I Feel:

I Am Getting Better At:

Today I Figured Out:

Today Was:

My Body Needs:

Today's Compliment To Myself:

I Know I Can:

Today's Story:

Today I Prayed:

My Baby:

The Best Advice Given To Me....

NEW MAMA THOUGHTS

THE NEXT 60 DAYS: I'M EVOLVING

Date:

Mood:

I Feel:

Today I Figured Out:

My Body Needs:

I Know I Can:

Today I Prayed:

I Am Getting Better At:

Today Was:

Today's Compliment To Myself:

Today's Story:

My Baby:

THE NEXT 60 DAYS: I'M EVOLVING

Date:

Mood:

I Feel:

Today I Figured Out:

My Body Needs:

I Know I Can:

Today I Prayed:

I Am Getting Better At:

Today Was:

Today's Compliment To Myself:

Today's Story:

My Baby:

THE NEXT 60 DAYS: I'M EVOLVING

Date:

Mood:

I Feel:

Today I Figured Out:

My Body Needs:

I Know I Can:

Today I Prayed:

I Am Getting Better At:

Today Was:

Today's Compliment To Myself:

Today's Story:

My Baby:

THE NEXT 60 DAYS: I'M EVOLVING

Date:

Mood:

I Feel:

I Am Getting Better At:

Today I Figured Out:

Today Was:

My Body Needs:

Today's Compliment To Myself:

I Know I Can:

Today's Story:

Today I Prayed:

My Baby:

I Release My Need To Control Everything. I Know God Is Taking Care Of Me And My Baby.

THE NEXT 60 DAYS: I'M EVOLVING

Date:

Mood:

I Feel:

Today I Figured Out:

My Body Needs:

I Know I Can:

Today I Prayed:

I Am Getting Better At:

Today Was:

Today's Compliment To Myself:

Today's Story:

My Baby:

Letting The Day Flow. I Will Not Push Against It. I Will Flow With It.

Dishes
Aren't
Wash And
Laundry
Isn't Done.
That's Okay.

THE NEXT 60 DAYS: I'M EVOLVING

Date:

Mood:

I Feel:

I Am Getting Better At:

Today I Figured Out:

Today Was:

My Body Needs:

Today's Compliment To Myself:

I Know I Can:

Today's Story:

Today I Prayed:

My Baby:

THE NEXT 60 DAYS: I'M EVOLVING

Date:

Mood:

I Feel:

Today I Figured Out:

My Body Needs:

I Know I Can:

Today I Prayed:

I Am Getting Better At:

Today Was:

Today's Compliment To Myself:

Today's Story:

My Baby:

My Group Of Friends....

THE NEXT 60 DAYS: I'M EVOLVING

Date:

Mood:

I Feel:

I Am Getting Better At:

Today I Figured Out:

Today Was:

My Body Needs:

Today's Compliment To Myself:

I Know I Can:

Today's Story:

Today I Prayed:

My Baby:

THE NEXT 60 DAYS: I'M EVOLVING

Date:

Mood:

I Feel:

Today I Figured Out:

My Body Needs:

I Know I Can:

Today I Prayed:

I Am Getting Better At:

Today Was:

Today's Compliment To Myself:

Today's Story:

My Baby:

THE NEXT 60 DAYS: I'M EVOLVING

Date:

Mood:

I Feel:

Today I Figured Out:

My Body Needs:

I Know I Can:

Today I Prayed:

I Am Getting Better At:

Today Was:

Today's Compliment To Myself:

Today's Story:

My Baby:

THE NEXT 60 DAYS: I'M EVOLVING

Date:

Mood:

I Feel:

I Am Getting Better At:

Today I Figured Out:

Today Was:

My Body Needs:

Today's Compliment To Myself:

I Know I Can:

Today's Story:

Today I Prayed:

My Baby:

I Am Energetic And Filled With Love And Enthusiasm.

NEW MAMA THOUGHTS

I Can't Keep My Eyes Off Of The Beauty That I Call My Baby.

THE NEXT 60 DAYS: I'M EVOLVING

Date:

Mood:

I Feel:

I Am Getting Better At:

Today I Figured Out:

Today Was:

My Body Needs:

Today's Compliment To Myself:

I Know I Can:

Today's Story:

Today I Prayed:

My Baby:

THE NEXT 60 DAYS: I'M EVOLVING

Date:

Mood:

I Feel:

I Am Getting Better At:

Today I Figured Out:

Today Was:

My Body Needs:

Today's Compliment To Myself:

I Know I Can:

Today's Story:

Today I Prayed:

My Baby:

THE NEXT 60 DAYS: I'M EVOLVING

Date:

Mood:

I Feel:

Today I Figured Out:

My Body Needs:

I Know I Can:

Today I Prayed:

I Am Getting Better At:

Today Was:

Today's Compliment To Myself:

Today's Story:

My Baby:

THE NEXT 60 DAYS: I'M EVOLVING

Date:

Mood:

I Feel:

Today I Figured Out:

My Body Needs:

I Know I Can:

Today I Prayed:

I Am Getting Better At:

Today Was:

Today's Compliment To Myself:

Today's Story:

My Baby:

Advice I Would Give To Other Mothers....

Stop
Freaking
Out.
You've
Got This.

It's Okay
If They
Underestimate
Me.
My Comeback
Will Be
Amazing.

THE NEXT 60 DAYS: I'M EVOLVING

Date:

I Feel:

Today I Figured Out:

My Body Needs:

I Know I Can:

Today I Prayed:

Mood:

I Am Getting Better At:

Today Was:

Today's Compliment To Myself:

Today's Story:

My Baby:

THE NEXT 60 DAYS: I'M EVOLVING

Date:

Mood:

I Feel:

Today I Figured Out:

My Body Needs:

I Know I Can:

Today I Prayed:

I Am Getting Better At:

Today Was:

Today's Compliment To Myself:

Today's Story:

My Baby:

THE NEXT 60 DAYS: I'M EVOLVING

Date:

Mood:

I Feel:

I Am Getting Better At:

Today I Figured Out:

Today Was:

My Body Needs:

Today's Compliment To Myself:

I Know I Can:

Today's Story:

Today I Prayed:

My Baby:

Mistakes I Need To Forgive Myself For....

THE NEXT 60 DAYS: I'M EVOLVING

Date:

Mood:

I Feel:

Today I Figured Out:

My Body Needs:

I Know I Can:

Today I Prayed:

I Am Getting Better At:

Today Was:

Today's Compliment To Myself:

Today's Story:

My Baby:

THE NEXT 60 DAYS: I'M EVOLVING

Date:

Mood:

I Feel:

Today I Figured Out:

My Body Needs:

I Know I Can:

Today I Prayed:

I Am Getting Better At:

Today Was:

Today's Compliment To Myself:

Today's Story:

My Baby:

It May Not Get Easy But It Does Get Better. I Am Growing Through It Baby!!!

All That Crying Means That Some Days I Am Loved A Little Louder Than Others.

THE NEXT 60 DAYS: I'M EVOLVING

Date:

Mood:

I Feel:

I Am Getting Better At:

Today I Figured Out:

Today Was:

My Body Needs:

Today's Compliment To Myself:

I Know I Can:

Today's Story:

Today I Prayed:

My Baby:

THE NEXT 60 DAYS: I'M EVOLVING

Date:

Mood:

I Feel:

Today I Figured Out:

My Body Needs:

I Know I Can:

Today I Prayed:

I Am Getting Better At:

Today Was:

Today's Compliment To Myself:

Today's Story:

My Baby:

NEW MAMA THOUGHTS

THE NEXT 60 DAYS: I'M EVOLVING

Date:

Mood:

I Feel:

Today I Figured Out:

My Body Needs:

I Know I Can:

Today I Prayed:

I Am Getting Better At:

Today Was:

Today's Compliment To Myself:

Today's Story:

My Baby:

THE NEXT 60 DAYS: I'M EVOLVING

Date:

Mood:

I Feel:

Today I Figured Out:

My Body Needs:

I Know I Can:

Today I Prayed:

I Am Getting Better At:

Today Was:

Today's Compliment To Myself:

Today's Story:

My Baby:

THE NEXT 60 DAYS: I'M EVOLVING

Date:

Mood:

I Feel:

Today I Figured Out:

My Body Needs:

I Know I Can:

Today I Prayed:

I Am Getting Better At:

Today Was:

Today's Compliment To Myself:

Today's Story:

My Baby:

A Letter To Myself A Year From Today....

THE NEXT 60 DAYS: I'M EVOLVING

Date:

Mood:

I Feel:

Today I Figured Out:

My Body Needs:

I Know I Can:

Today I Prayed:

I Am Getting Better At:

Today Was:

Today's Compliment To Myself:

Today's Story:

My Baby:

THE NEXT 60 DAYS: I'M EVOLVING

Date:

Mood:

I Feel:

Today I Figured Out:

My Body Needs:

I Know I Can:

Today I Prayed:

I Am Getting Better At:

Today Was:

Today's Compliment To Myself:

Today's Story:

My Baby:

NEW MAMA THOUGHTS

THE NEXT 60 DAYS: I'M EVOLVING

Date:

Mood:

I Feel:

I Am Getting Better At:

Today I Figured Out:

Today Was:

My Body Needs:

Today's Compliment To Myself:

I Know I Can:

Today's Story:

Today I Prayed:

My Baby:

It's Not About Being Perfect. It's About Showing Up And Doing My Best.

THESE 60 DAYS:

LET'S TALK BONDING

THESE 60 DAYS: LET'S TALK BONDING

Date:

Mood:

I Feel:

Today I Worried Less About:

Today I Asked Myself:

It Is Getting Easier To:

The Answer To The Above Question:

Today Was:

I Am Inspired To:

Today's Story:

My Baby:____

THESE 60 DAYS: LET'S TALK BONDING

Date: Mood:

I Feel:

Today I Worried Less About:

Today I Asked Myself:

It Is Getting Easier To:

The Answer To The Above Question:

Today Was:

I Am Inspired To:

Today's Story:

My Baby:____

I Fully Accept What Is Happening Right Now.

THESE 60 DAYS: LET'S TALK BONDING

Date:

Mood:

I Feel:

Today I Asked Myself:

The Answer To The Above Question:

I Am Inspired To:

Today I Worried Less About:

It Is Getting Easier To:

Today Was:

Today's Story:

My Baby:____

I Trust My Ability To Be A Wonderful And Loving Mother.

Somedays
I Want To
Give Up,
But Today
I'm Glad I
Didn't.

I No Longer Feel Bad Because I Know I'm Not Doing All Of This By Myself.

THESE 60 DAYS: LET'S TALK BONDING

Date:

Mood:

I Feel:

Today I Asked Myself:

The Answer To The Above Question:

I Am Inspired To:

Today I Worried Less About:

It Is Getting Easier To:

Today Was:

Today's Story:

My Baby:____

I Trust My Ability To Make The Right Parenting Decisions And Choices.

THESE 60 DAYS: LET'S TALK BONDING

Date:

Mood:

I Feel:

Today I Asked Myself:

The Answer To The Above Question:

I Am Inspired To:

Today I Worried Less About:

It Is Getting Easier To:

Today Was:

Today's Story:

My Baby:____

THESE 60 DAYS: LET'S TALK BONDING

Date:

Mood:

I Feel:

Today I Asked Myself:

The Answer To The Above Question:

I Am Inspired To:

Today I Worried Less About:

It Is Getting Easier To:

Today Was:

Today's Story:

My Baby:______________________________

NEW MAMA THOUGHTS

I Didn't Lose
A Part Of
Myself.
I Just Gained
A New
Extension Of
Myself.

Everyday We Are Growing More And More Attached To Each Other.

THESE 60 DAYS: LET'S TALK BONDING

Date:

Mood:

I Feel:

Today I Asked Myself:

The Answer To The Above Question:

I Am Inspired To:

Today I Worried Less About:

It Is Getting Easier To:

Today Was:

Today's Story:

My Baby:______________________________

THESE 60 DAYS: LET'S TALK BONDING

Date:

Mood:

I Feel:

Today I Worried Less About:

Today I Asked Myself:

It Is Getting Easier To:

The Answer To The Above Question:

Today Was:

I Am Inspired To:

Today's Story:

My Baby:____

THESE 60 DAYS: LET'S TALK BONDING

Date:

Mood:

I Feel:

Today I Asked Myself:

The Answer To The Above Question:

I Am Inspired To:

Today I Worried Less About:

It Is Getting Easier To:

Today Was:

Today's Story:

My Baby:______________________________

It's Very Therapeutic For Me To....

THESE 60 DAYS: LET'S TALK BONDING

Date:

Mood:

I Feel:

Today I Asked Myself:

The Answer To The Above Question:

I Am Inspired To:

Today I Worried Less About:

It Is Getting Easier To:

Today Was:

Today's Story:

My Baby:____

I Trust My Maternal Intuition And Its Ability To Lead Me Towards The Right Path.

THESE 60 DAYS: LET'S TALK BONDING

Date:

Mood:

I Feel:

Today I Asked Myself:

The Answer To The Above Question:

I Am Inspired To:

Today I Worried Less About:

It Is Getting Easier To:

Today Was:

Today's Story:

My Baby:____

The Old Me Is Embracing The New Me With Love.

THESE 60 DAYS: LET'S TALK BONDING

Date:

Mood:

I Feel:

Today I Asked Myself:

The Answer To The Above Question:

I Am Inspired To:

Today I Worried Less About:

It Is Getting Easier To:

Today Was:

Today's Story:

My Baby:____

THESE 60 DAYS: LET'S TALK BONDING

Date:

Mood:

I Feel:

Today I Asked Myself:

The Answer To The Above Question:

I Am Inspired To:

Today I Worried Less About:

It Is Getting Easier To:

Today Was:

Today's Story:

My Baby:____

THESE 60 DAYS: LET'S TALK BONDING

Date:

Mood:

I Feel:

Today I Asked Myself:

The Answer To The Above Question:

I Am Inspired To:

Today I Worried Less About:

It Is Getting Easier To:

Today Was:

Today's Story:

My Baby:____

I Love
To Love
All
Over My
Baby.

Creating More Happiness By Celebrating My Small Victories.

THESE 60 DAYS: LET'S TALK BONDING

Date:

Mood:

I Feel:

Today I Asked Myself:

The Answer To The Above Question:

I Am Inspired To:

Today I Worried Less About:

It Is Getting Easier To:

Today Was:

Today's Story:

My Baby:____

THESE 60 DAYS: LET'S TALK BONDING

Date:

Mood:

I Feel:

Today I Worried Less About:

Today I Asked Myself:

It Is Getting Easier To:

The Answer To The Above Question:

Today Was:

I Am Inspired To:

Today's Story:

My Baby:____

THESE 60 DAYS: LET'S TALK BONDING

Date: Mood:

I Feel:	Today I Worried Less About:
Today I Asked Myself:	It Is Getting Easier To:
The Answer To The Above Question:	Today Was:
I Am Inspired To:	Today's Story:

My Baby:____

THESE 60 DAYS: LET'S TALK BONDING

Date:

Mood:

I Feel:

Today I Asked Myself:

The Answer To The Above Question:

I Am Inspired To:

Today I Worried Less About:

It Is Getting Easier To:

Today Was:

Today's Story:

My Baby:____

NEW MAMA THOUGHTS

THESE 60 DAYS: LET'S TALK BONDING

Date:

Mood:

I Feel:

Today I Asked Myself:

The Answer To The Above Question:

I Am Inspired To:

Today I Worried Less About:

It Is Getting Easier To:

Today Was:

Today's Story:

My Baby:____

THESE 60 DAYS: LET'S TALK BONDING

Date: Mood:

I Feel:

Today I Asked Myself:

The Answer To The Above Question:

I Am Inspired To:

Today I Worried Less About:

It Is Getting Easier To:

Today Was:

Today's Story:

My Baby:________________________________

THESE 60 DAYS: LET'S TALK BONDING

Date:

Mood:

I Feel:

Today I Asked Myself:

The Answer To The Above Question:

I Am Inspired To:

Today I Worried Less About:

It Is Getting Easier To:

Today Was:

Today's Story:

My Baby:____

Forgiving Myself For Not Being Perfect. Loving Myself For Every Attempt To Be.

I Know
I Am
Blossoming
In This
Season.

THESE 60 DAYS: LET'S TALK BONDING

Date:

Mood:

I Feel:

Today I Worried Less About:

Today I Asked Myself:

It Is Getting Easier To:

The Answer To The Above Question:

Today Was:

I Am Inspired To:

Today's Story:

My Baby:____

THESE 60 DAYS: LET'S TALK BONDING

Date:

Mood:

I Feel:

Today I Asked Myself:

The Answer To The Above Question:

I Am Inspired To:

Today I Worried Less About:

It Is Getting Easier To:

Today Was:

Today's Story:

My Baby:____

THESE 60 DAYS: LET'S TALK BONDING

Date: Mood:

I Feel:

Today I Worried Less About:

Today I Asked Myself:

It Is Getting Easier To:

The Answer To The Above Question:

Today Was:

I Am Inspired To:

Today's Story:

My Baby:____

NEW MAMA THOUGHTS

My New Baby Has Inspired My Passion To/For....

THESE 60 DAYS: LET'S TALK BONDING

Date:

Mood:

I Feel:

Today I Asked Myself:

The Answer To The Above Question:

I Am Inspired To:

Today I Worried Less About:

It Is Getting Easier To:

Today Was:

Today's Story:

My Baby:____

I Choose To Create A Peaceful And Harmonious Environment Filled With Love For The Whole Family.

THESE 60 DAYS: LET'S TALK BONDING

Date:

Mood:

I Feel:

Today I Asked Myself:

The Answer To The Above Question:

I Am Inspired To:

Today I Worried Less About:

It Is Getting Easier To:

Today Was:

Today's Story:

My Baby:____

THESE 60 DAYS: LET'S TALK BONDING

Date:

Mood:

I Feel:

Today I Asked Myself:

The Answer To The Above Question:

I Am Inspired To:

Today I Worried Less About:

It Is Getting Easier To:

Today Was:

Today's Story:

My Baby:____

My Ideal Day With My Family Looks And Feels Like....

THESE 60 DAYS: LET'S TALK BONDING

Date:

Mood:

I Feel:

Today I Asked Myself:

The Answer To The Above Question:

I Am Inspired To:

Today I Worried Less About:

It Is Getting Easier To:

Today Was:

Today's Story:

My Baby:____

THESE 60 DAYS: LET'S TALK BONDING

Date: Mood:

I Feel:

Today I Asked Myself:

The Answer To The Above Question:

I Am Inspired To:

Today I Worried Less About:

It Is Getting Easier To:

Today Was:

Today's Story:

My Baby:____

Women
Are
Powerful
Warriors.

THESE 60 DAYS: LET'S TALK BONDING

Date:

Mood:

I Feel:

Today I Asked Myself:

The Answer To The Above Question:

I Am Inspired To:

Today I Worried Less About:

It Is Getting Easier To:

Today Was:

Today's Story:

My Baby:____

THESE 60 DAYS: LET'S TALK BONDING

Date:

Mood:

I Feel:

Today I Asked Myself:

The Answer To The Above Question:

I Am Inspired To:

Today I Worried Less About:

It Is Getting Easier To:

Today Was:

Today's Story:

My Baby:____

THESE 60 DAYS: LET'S TALK BONDING

Date:

Mood:

I Feel:

Today I Asked Myself:

The Answer To The Above Question:

I Am Inspired To:

Today I Worried Less About:

It Is Getting Easier To:

Today Was:

Today's Story:

My Baby:____

Loving Myself Through It All.

NEW MAMA THOUGHTS

As A Mom, I Choose To Handle All Of My Responsibilities With Confidence And Grace.

THESE 60 DAYS: LET'S TALK BONDING

Date:

Mood:

I Feel:

Today I Worried Less About:

Today I Asked Myself:

It Is Getting Easier To:

The Answer To The Above Question:

Today Was:

I Am Inspired To:

Today's Story:

My Baby:____

THESE 60 DAYS: LET'S TALK BONDING

Date: Mood:

I Feel:

Today I Worried Less About:

Today I Asked Myself:

It Is Getting Easier To:

The Answer To The Above Question:

Today Was:

I Am Inspired To:

Today's Story:

My Baby:____

THESE 60 DAYS: LET'S TALK BONDING

Date: Mood:

I Feel:

Today I Worried Less About:

Today I Asked Myself:

It Is Getting Easier To:

The Answer To The Above Question:

Today Was:

I Am Inspired To:

Today's Story:

My Baby:____

I Am Stronger Than I Think.

Things
Will Get
Better.

THESE 60 DAYS: LET'S TALK BONDING

Date:

Mood:

I Feel:

Today I Worried Less About:

Today I Asked Myself:

It Is Getting Easier To:

The Answer To The Above Question:

Today Was:

I Am Inspired To:

Today's Story:

My Baby:____

I Give Myself Permission To Pause And Take A Breather From Time To Time.

THESE 60 DAYS: LET'S TALK BONDING

Date:

Mood:

I Feel:

Today I Asked Myself:

The Answer To The Above Question:

I Am Inspired To:

Today I Worried Less About:

It Is Getting Easier To:

Today Was:

Today's Story:

My Baby:____

THESE 60 DAYS: LET'S TALK BONDING

Date:

Mood:

I Feel:

Today I Asked Myself:

The Answer To The Above Question:

I Am Inspired To:

Today I Worried Less About:

It Is Getting Easier To:

Today Was:

Today's Story:

My Baby:____

I Am Predicting That The Next Three Months Will Be....

NEW MAMA THOUGHTS

THESE 60 DAYS: LET'S TALK BONDING

Date:

Mood:

I Feel:

Today I Asked Myself:

The Answer To The Above Question:

I Am Inspired To:

Today I Worried Less About:

It Is Getting Easier To:

Today Was:

Today's Story:

My Baby:____

THESE 60 DAYS: LET'S TALK BONDING

Date:

Mood:

I Feel:

Today I Asked Myself:

The Answer To The Above Question:

I Am Inspired To:

Today I Worried Less About:

It Is Getting Easier To:

Today Was:

Today's Story:

My Baby:____

I Have A Strong Connection With My Child.

THESE 60 DAYS: LET'S TALK BONDING

Date:

Mood:

I Feel:

Today I Asked Myself:

The Answer To The Above Question:

I Am Inspired To:

Today I Worried Less About:

It Is Getting Easier To:

Today Was:

Today's Story:

My Baby:____

God Has Shown Me The Highest Form Of Love Through My Baby.

THESE 60 DAYS: LET'S TALK BONDING

Date:

Mood:

I Feel:

Today I Asked Myself:

The Answer To The Above Question:

I Am Inspired To:

Today I Worried Less About:

It Is Getting Easier To:

Today Was:

Today's Story:

My Baby:____

THESE 60 DAYS: LET'S TALK BONDING

Date: Mood:

I Feel:

Today I Worried Less About:

Today I Asked Myself:

It Is Getting Easier To:

The Answer To The Above Question:

Today Was:

I Am Inspired To:

Today's Story:

My Baby:____

THESE 60 DAYS: LET'S TALK BONDING

Date:

Mood:

I Feel:

Today I Worried Less About:

Today I Asked Myself:

It Is Getting Easier To:

The Answer To The Above Question:

Today Was:

I Am Inspired To:

Today's Story:

My Baby:____

THESE 60 DAYS: LET'S TALK BONDING

Date:

Mood:

I Feel:

Today I Asked Myself:

The Answer To The Above Question:

I Am Inspired To:

Today I Worried Less About:

It Is Getting Easier To:

Today Was:

Today's Story:

My Baby:______________________________

A Safe Person I Can Talk To About My Feelings And/Or Daily Struggles....

NEW MAMA THOUGHTS

THESE 60 DAYS: LET'S TALK BONDING

Date:

Mood:

I Feel:

Today I Worried Less About:

Today I Asked Myself:

It Is Getting Easier To:

The Answer To The Above Question:

Today Was:

I Am Inspired To:

Today's Story:

My Baby:____

THESE 60 DAYS: LET'S TALK BONDING

Date:

Mood:

I Feel:

Today I Asked Myself:

The Answer To The Above Question:

I Am Inspired To:

Today I Worried Less About:

It Is Getting Easier To:

Today Was:

Today's Story:

My Baby:______________________________

I Have A Strong Will And Determination To Make Motherhood Work.

THESE 60 DAYS: LET'S TALK BONDING

Date:

Mood:

I Feel:

Today I Asked Myself:

The Answer To The Above Question:

I Am Inspired To:

Today I Worried Less About:

It Is Getting Easier To:

Today Was:

Today's Story:

My Baby:____

I Enjoy Fulfilling My Duties And Responsibilities As A Mother. I Never See This Role As A Burden.

Scary Thoughts I Have Towards My Baby....

THESE 60 DAYS: LET'S TALK BONDING

Date:

Mood:

I Feel:

Today I Asked Myself:

The Answer To The Above Question:

I Am Inspired To:

Today I Worried Less About:

It Is Getting Easier To:

Today Was:

Today's Story:

My Baby:____

THESE 60 DAYS: LET'S TALK BONDING

Date:

Mood:

I Feel:

Today I Asked Myself:

The Answer To The Above Question:

I Am Inspired To:

Today I Worried Less About:

It Is Getting Easier To:

Today Was:

Today's Story:

My Baby:____

THESE 60 DAYS: LET'S TALK BONDING

Date:

Mood:

I Feel:

Today I Asked Myself:

The Answer To The Above Question:

I Am Inspired To:

Today I Worried Less About:

It Is Getting Easier To:

Today Was:

Today's Story:

My Baby:____

THESE 60 DAYS: LET'S TALK BONDING

Date:

Mood:

I Feel:

Today I Asked Myself:

The Answer To The Above Question:

I Am Inspired To:

Today I Worried Less About:

It Is Getting Easier To:

Today Was:

Today's Story:

My Baby:______________________________

Who Am I Outside Of Being A Mom?

NEW MAMA THOUGHTS

THESE 60 DAYS: LET'S TALK BONDING

Date:

Mood:

I Feel:

Today I Asked Myself:

The Answer To The Above Question:

I Am Inspired To:

Today I Worried Less About:

It Is Getting Easier To:

Today Was:

Today's Story:

My Baby:____

THESE 60 DAYS: LET'S TALK BONDING

Date:

Mood:

I Feel:

Today I Asked Myself:

The Answer To The Above Question:

I Am Inspired To:

Today I Worried Less About:

It Is Getting Easier To:

Today Was:

Today's Story:

My Baby:____

I Find A Reason To Laugh Everyday.

THESE 60 DAYS: LET'S TALK BONDING

Date:

Mood:

I Feel:

Today I Asked Myself:

The Answer To The Above Question:

I Am Inspired To:

Today I Worried Less About:

It Is Getting Easier To:

Today Was:

Today's Story:

My Baby:____

I Am A
Mother
Because
I Serve
And Give.

Mommy
Life Is
The Best
Life.

THESE 60 DAYS: LET'S TALK BONDING

Date:

Mood:

I Feel:

Today I Worried Less About:

Today I Asked Myself:

It Is Getting Easier To:

The Answer To The Above Question:

Today Was:

I Am Inspired To:

Today's Story:

My Baby:____

My Baby Uplifts Me. Just Seeing My Baby Is Enough To Brighten My Day.

THESE 60 DAYS: LET'S TALK BONDING

Date:

Mood:

I Feel:

Today I Asked Myself:

The Answer To The Above Question:

I Am Inspired To:

Today I Worried Less About:

It Is Getting Easier To:

Today Was:

Today's Story:

My Baby:____

If I Am Being Honest With Myself, I Would Say....

Five Things I Believe That I Am Missing Out On....

1.

2.

3.

4.

5.

THESE 60 DAYS: LET'S TALK BONDING

Date: Mood:

I Feel:

Today I Worried Less About:

Today I Asked Myself:

It Is Getting Easier To:

The Answer To The Above Question:

Today Was:

I Am Inspired To:

Today's Story:

My Baby:____

THESE 60 DAYS: LET'S TALK BONDING

Date:

Mood:

I Feel:

Today I Asked Myself:

The Answer To The Above Question:

I Am Inspired To:

Today I Worried Less About:

It Is Getting Easier To:

Today Was:

Today's Story:

My Baby:____

NEW MAMA THOUGHTS

I Can't Wait Until My Body....

THESE 60 DAYS: LET'S TALK BONDING

Date:

Mood:

I Feel:

Today I Worried Less About:

Today I Asked Myself:

It Is Getting Easier To:

The Answer To The Above Question:

Today Was:

I Am Inspired To:

Today's Story:

My Baby:____

THESE 60 DAYS: LET'S TALK BONDING

Date:

Mood:

I Feel:

Today I Worried Less About:

Today I Asked Myself:

It Is Getting Easier To:

The Answer To The Above Question:

Today Was:

I Am Inspired To:

Today's Story:

My Baby:____

In Being A Mom, I Find That I Am More Me Than I Have Ever Been.

Made in the USA
Columbia, SC
09 November 2019